VIENNA

137 colour photographs with city map

Getting to know Vienna is certainly one of the most pleasant pastimes that a person travelling in Europe can enjoy. Its many facets, its important sights, its hidden secrets — all comprise Vienna's enchanting atmosphere that visitors find difficult to resist.

Due to both its political and geographical position in the heart of Europe, Vienna has been influenced by a wide diversity of factors since its earliest days. Here, ethnical and cultural, political and social streams of thought collided with or melted into one another, disappeared entirely or were carried to the furthest corners of the world. The variety of influences which determined the development of modern Vienna, and the multitude of factors which emitted from this city to influence the world, shall become clearer by taking a closer look at this city's colourful history.

Vienna is one of the oldest settlements of the European capital cities. The Celts already resided here centuries before the birth of Christ. In the year 1 AD, the Romans established the fortifications known as "Vindobona", which, until the mighty waves of immigration, continued to play a vital role within the Roman "Limes" or fortified walls.

In the Annals of Salzburg from 881 AD, reference is made of "Wenia" (the origin of this name, however, is unexplained). The Babenbergs, the first dynasty to reign over Austria, chose Vienna, which was first deemed "city" in 1137, as their residence in 1155. During the reigns of Leopold V and Leopold VI, who was also known as "Leopold the Glorious", Vienna underwent considerable expansion. These activities were financed primarily with the ransom of one million German marks that the English were forced to pay to the Babenbergs for the return of the captured King Richard the Lionhearted.

Soon after the last Babenberg was killed during the battle against the Hungarian Army in 1246, Ottocar II Przemysl of Bohemia was given control of Austria, which in turn was violently taken from him by Rudolf I of Hapsburg at the Battle of Dürnkrut in 1278. Though the citizens of Vienna, who favoured King Ottocar, were less than enthusiastic about being ruled by the Hapsburgs, the latter reigned for the next 600 years. The city lost almost all of its privileges after the rebellion of 1288.

Despite those circumstances, Vienna enjoyed tremendous growth throughout the 14th century, its population amounting to around 40,000 inhabitants. Rudolf IV, the Founder, established the University of Vienna (the oldest university in today's German-speaking territory) and had significant influence on the Gothic-style expansion of Vienna's distinctive landmark, the St. Stephen's Cathedral (the "Stephansdom"). Early in the 16th century, the citizens of Vienna renewed their struggles against the Hapsburg rule; this rebellion was paid for dearly with the lives of five mayors and a significant decrease in the city's political and economic spheres of influence. Under the military leadership of Count Salm, Vienna was victorious in the first defensive battle against the Turkish invaders.

At the end of the 16th century, an intense wave of counter-reformationism swept over the people of Vienna, the majority of whom were Protestant in their beliefs. In 1683, Prince Eugene of Savoy, with military support from Bavaria, Saxony and Poland, withstood the second attempt of the Turks to claim Vienna, thus preventing their further advance into the European continent.

The baroque construction boom following the liberation from the Turkish oppressors and which took place primarily during the reigns of Emperor Charles VI and Empress Maria Theresia (who commissioned many famous architects such as Lukas von Hildebrandt and the father and son of the Fischer von Erlach family), resulted in the Austrian capital being given the title of "Glorious Vienna". Vienna acquired international renown as a city of music in the late 18th and early 19th centuries, when musicians such as Joseph Haydn, Wolfgang Amadeus Mozart and Ludwig van Beethoven made their marks on the "Viennese Classical Era".

After the Napoleonic Wars, during which Vienna was twice occupied by French troops, representatives of Europe's leading powers, under the leadership of Prince Metternich, gathered in Vienna in 1814—1815 for the Congress of Vienna to negotiate the new territorial divisions of the continent. In the years of the political Restoration which followed, Austria suffered under both Metternich's repressive police state and the emerging social tensions caused by the beginnings of industrialization. During the year of the 1848 Revolution, the citizens of Austria once again vented their dissatisfaction in a number of revolts; Prince Metternich was overthrown and Emperor Ferdinand was forced to abdicate. Emperor Francis Joseph assumed the throne and was to reign for the next 68 years.

After the ancient city walls were razed in 1857, numerous representative buildings were built along the almost 200-foot-wide (60-metre-wide) "Ring".

In 1873, the year of the World Exposition, the stock market crash paralyzed the business world and contributed to the widespread impoverishment of the people.

Around the turn of the century, Vienna provided an excellent setting for outstanding cultural and scientific achievements in the fields of medicine (Sigmund Freud, Theodor Billroth), literature (Arthur Schnitzler, Stefan Zweig, Karl Kraus), architecture (Otto Wagner, Adolf Loos), art (Gustav Klimt, Egon Schiele) and music (Arnold Schönberg, Alban Berg, Anton von Webern).

At the end of World War I, Vienna was no longer the metropolis of a gigantic empire, but rather it and its almost two million inhabitants had become the far-too-large capital city of the tiny, barely viable new state of Austria. Despite the over 60,000 social housing units provided by the government in the period between the wars, social differences were maintained and even augmented. In 1938, Adolf Hitler's army marched into an Austria fraught with social and political tensions. After almost one-fifth of Vienna's buildings had been destroyed by bombs during the last year of the war, the Allied troops finally freed the city in the spring of 1945. The ten subsequent years of occupation were brought to an end when Federal Chancellor Figl signed the State Treaty and proclaimed "Austria is free!" from the balcony of the Belvedere Palace in 1955.

Vienna can thank the "permanent neutrality of Austria" which was founded in that treaty for its achieving the role as one of the most important meeting points between the East and West. Here one can find not only the headquarters of the International Atomic Energy Organization (IAEO) and the United Nations' Industrial Development Organization (UNIDO), but as of 1979, Vienna also became the third seat of the United Nations, in addition to New York and Geneva.

In Vienna, one senses the history, the touch of the past, much more intensely than in other cities. Perhaps this feeling is transmitted by the numerous architectural structures which provide stony testimony of the past. But more than that, it is the people of Vienna who enjoy nostalgically looking back into the past and conjuring up the period of the Austrian Empire. Apparently, they are only gradually becoming used to the fact that Vienna, in its role as the capital city of a small nation, has maintained its respected position among the other leading cities of Europe as a modern, active metropolis with a thriving cultural life. Today, the visitor to

Vienna can choose between the "Burgtheater" and one of the many modern "free group" theatres, can enjoy a classic Viennese coffee house or a "New Wave" bar, relish the world-famous acoustics of Vienna's Music Society Hall or the dim atmosphere of a jazz club ... old and new, classical and *avante-garde*, all existing side by side.

Let us remain with the inhabitants of this city for a while. The "typical Viennese" personality is the subject of numerous clichés, facades which either represent that famous grain of truth or try to hide just the opposite. According to the Brockhaus Encyclopedia, we will discover that the Viennese are a "sensuous, open-minded and cosmopolitan, likeable, 'gemütlich', nonchalant and light-hearted" people. It must be the sum of these characteristics which produces the almost proverbial phenomenon of Viennese charm — a quality which the Viennese possess in great quantities but which is far too precious to be displayed continuously. The picture of the grumpy, whining, servile-devout Viennese, with his penchant for the morbid, has been presented by Karl Kraus, Helmut Qualtinger and several other literary figures of this city, which has borne its own most severe critics. The latter all had or have one feature in common — they "can't stand it in Vienna, nor anywhere else in the world", (Qualtinger). And since the typical Viennese has a prediliction for criticizing that which he loves the most, there is always plenty of material to find in his home city.

A somewhat unbalanced relationship exists between the Viennese and their countrymen, or better said provincial "country cousins". The friendliness of the feelings toward the capital city and its inhabitants decreases exponentially the further one gets from that metropolis — beyond a certain distance, Vienna and the Viennese are, in fact, considered somewhat superfluous by other Austrians. This attitude, however, does not diminish the amicable sentiments which the Viennese consistantly maintain toward the provinces. However, should a situation become too "provincial", no Viennese tries to hide the fact that he is from the "big city" from the "Gscherten" (transl.: "shorn heads"; short hair was indicative of rural inhabitants in earlier days).

Defining features of "typical Vienna" is even more difficult than attempting to capture the nature of its inhabitants. Coffee houses and pastries, New Year's Concert and the Opera Ball, *art nouveau* and baroque architecture, St. Stephen's Cathedral, the Prater Amusement Park, "Fiaker" — the famous horsedrawn carriages, the Vienna Choir Boys and the Spanish Riding School, the atmosphere of a "Heuriger" where new wine is served and Viennese melodies can be heard — all play a vital role in the picture of this city. A multitude of other secrets are just waiting to be discovered — hidden behind this wall of clichés. Experience the familiar and the unknown for yourself to make this stay in Vienna an adventure to be remembered for years to come. This brochure has been designed to provide some modest support in achieving that goal.

The landmark of Vienna, the **St. Stephen's Cathedral** ("Stephansdom"), is considered one of Europe's most well-known churches and is also Austria's most important example of Gothic architecture. Its history began in 1140, when the Bishop of Passau, who had jurisdiction over the Viennese churches at that time, ordered the construction of a new parish church outside of the existing city walls. The Romanesque structure was dedicated to St. Stephen and consecrated in 1147. The church underwent almost complete renovation in the middle of the 13th century and became one of the last great Romanesque ecclesiastical structures within the German-speaking territories of Europe. Today, the cathedral's west facade, with its splendid portal and the two "Pagans' Towers" ("Heidentürme"), still provides evidence of the construction work carried out during that early period.

The Gothic reconstruction of the cathedral, with its three naves and High Gothic choir hall, commenced in 1304; it was consecrated 36 years later. In 1359, Rudolf IV, the Founder, initiated the construction of both the south tower, which, with a height of over 450 ft (136.7 m), is the third-highest church tower in the world, and the Late Gothic nave. These were simply built around the existing Romanesque church. After the razing of the Romanesque nave, which began in 1426, the construction of the Gothic walls could be commenced. By the end of the 15th century, the roof structure provided an outstanding example of Gothic woodworking mastery. Work on the north tower was discontinued in 1511 when the structure was only half its intended height; building activities ceased entirely in 1523. At the end of the 16th century, a Renaissance-style octa-

gonal capped roof and a belfrey were added. The interior of the more than 360-foot-long (110 m) main nave of the cathedral is no less impressive than the view granted of the church from the outside. The **High Altar** (built between 1640 and 1647, shown at left) is a masterpiece created by the brothers Johann Jakob and Tobias Pock of Constance. The painting behind the alter, which depicts St. Stephen being stoned to death, was painted on a pewter surface which measures 300 ft² (28 m²) and is considered the latter brother's major work. The statues represent the saints Leopold and Florian (inside) and Sebastian and Rochus (outside).

The master stonemason, Anton Pilgram, immortalized himself in a stone bust at the lower end of the **organ base** which he created. On the banner beneath his self-portrait (shown above), he inscribed his initials and the date 1513. Aside from the sculpture's artistic value, it is a stony indication that the anonymity of artists that had prevailed throughout the Middle Ages was gradually disappearing.

The **"Wiener Neustädter Altar"** (pictured at bottom of previous page) was built in 1447 with a charitable donation from Frederick III, whose tomb is also found in the cathedral. The upper half of the central shrine of this magnificent example of the Alpine school of sculpture depicts Mary's Coronation; the lower half shows the Madonna with Child sitting on a throne. The frame of the shrine is decorated with statues of the Apostles. The sculptures on the left wing represent the Annunciation above and the Birth of Christ below. The upper section of the right wing presents the Visitation of Mary, the bottom scene shows the Three Wise Men. The "Andreasaltar", though not belonging to the winged shrine, has been placed on top of its central section.

The most outstanding piece of art in the nave is the splendid Late Gothic **pulpit** (pictured upper left), another of Anton Pilgram's sculptures, which was created at the beginning of the 16th century. Made out of seven blocks of sandstone, the four sides of the pulpit depict the four Early Fathers of the Latin Church: Augustinus, Pope Gregor the Great, Hieronymus and Ambrosius. The lizards and toads creeping up the stairwell symbolize evil, while the barking dog at the upper end of the banister, a symbol of goodness, prevents their advance. As he had done on the organ base, Pilgram again sculpted a self-portrait the so-called "Fenstergucker", (transl.: "Window Peeper", shown at left) on this magnificent pulpit.

The **Servant Madonna** ("Dienstbotenmadonna"), her name derived from an ancient legend, is found directly next to the pulpit. This statue, which depicts an ideal of religious hommage, provides a beautiful example of the high standard of sculpting artistry at the beginning of the 14th century. The equally beautiful **Caped Madonna** ("Schutzmantelmadonna", shown opposite, upper right) was created by an unknown artist around 100 to 150 years later.

The crypts, incorrectly entitled "catacombs", are located beneath the Albertina Choir Loft and are certainly worth viewing; the sarcophagi of several prominent persons such as Emperor Rudolf IV, the Founder, are also located there. A breathtaking view of the city is provided from the top of the south tower. The famous "Pummerin", a 20-ton bell and the largest church bell in Austria, hangs in the north tower; this bell is only rung on special occasions such as New Year's. During the devastating fire which almost demolished the cathedral in the last days of World War II, the bell fell from its lofty location and shattered; it was restored to its original position during the cathedral's seven-year-long reconstruction.

The baroque **Plague Column** ("Pest-säule") or "Holy Trinity Column" (shown opposite) was erected by Emperor Leopold I in fulfillment of an oath he made during the Plague epidemic in 1679. It is found on the **Graben** (shown above), which was the centre of city life during the Middle Ages.

At the corner of the Graben and Kärntner Strasse, one can find the **"Stock im Eisen"**, (pictured at left), the most legendary piece of wood in Vienna. The story began in the 16th century and explains that this trunk, a "larch-pine", is a remnant of a forest that once reached this site. The iron band which encircles the trunk is said to be unopenable. Innumerable sagas are also associated with the around 3,000 nails which have been hammered into the wood. At the beginning of this century, closer inspection showed that the wood is actually spruce and that the lock serves no purpose whatsoever!

Vienna's second oldest church with regard to its founding date is **St. Peter's Church** ("Peterskirche" — pictured above right). During the baroque period, the church was completely remodeled according to plans created by Lukas von Hildebrandt.

After the **Upper Market** ("Hohe Markt"), the oldest market place in Vienna, became too small at the end of the 12th century, the Babenbergs created a "novum forum": the **New Market** ("Neue Markt"). The latter soon developed into the centre of trade with the South as well as becoming the main exchange for grains and flour. In time, magnificent mansions, commercial establishments and townhouses — all in a unified style — were constructed on its periphery. For years, this was one of Vienna's most beautiful squares.

The Providentia Fountain (pictured above) is a work by George Raphael Donner for the City of Vienna, making it the first publicly funded fountain of purely secular nature. In 1770, Empress Maria Theresia ordered that the lead-cast nude figures be removed and given to the sculptor Martin Fischer to be melted down; the latter, however, recognized their artistic value and held them in safe keeping so that they could later be returned to their original site.

From 1633 on, members of the Imperial Court were buried in the **Capuchin Monastery Crypt** ("Kapuzinergruft"), which was donated by Emperor Matthias and his wife, Anna. Twelve emperors and fifteen empresses are included among those buried in the 138 metal coffins.

The **State Opera House** ("Staatsoper") was built between 1861 and 1869 according to the plans of architects Eduard van der Nüll and August Siccard von Siccardsburg. Even during its construction, the music theatre, built and furnished in French Renaissance style, was the subject of so much mockery and derision (with claims like, "neither Siccardsburg nor van der Nüll have any style at all") that neither architect lived to see the building completed — van der Nüll committed suicide and Siccardsburg died of a heart attack.

The Opera House was the first of the monumental buildings built on the Ring, the avenue which was created after the razing of the city wall in 1857. After its opening on May 25, 1869, with a presentation of Mozart's "Don Giovanni", the State Opera rapidly attained international status and firmly established Vienna's reputation as one of the world's leading music cities. The Vienna Philharmonic, the orchestra of the National Opera, enjoys as much international repute as the Opera's Ballet Company. The Opera Ball ("Opernball"), which is opened annually to the strains of the "Blue Danube Waltz" by hundreds of young pairs, is the culmination of the Carnival season in Vienna.

The **Albertina** houses the world's largest collection of graphic arts (approximately 40,000 drawings and water-colours and over one million prints). Included in the collection are works by Dürer, Rubens (an example shown in insert above), Holbein, Van Dyck, Michelangelo and Leonardo da Vinci.

The **Museum of Natural History** ("Naturhistorisches Museum" — shown above) and the **Museum of Fine Arts** ("Kunsthistorisches Museum" — opposite, above) are mirror images, placed facing one another on the outside periphery of the Ring. The architects, Semper and Hasenauer, designed them in Italian Renaissance style. The Museum of Natural History, somewhat simpler inside than its "twin", contains one of the largest natural history collections in Europe. Within the walls of the Museum of Fine Arts, one can not only visit the world's fourth-largest painting gallery but also view an impressive artistic handicrafts collection (which includes the golden salt receptacle created by Benvenuto Cellini, shown opposite, below).

A considerable proportion of the Museum's painting collection is dedicated to the works of Dutch, Old German, Flemish and English masters, primarily from the 16th to 18th centuries. In addition to the most famous works by Pieter Brueghel the Elder (including "A Country Wedding", "Building the Tower of Babel", "Children's Games" and "The Return of the Hunters", shown above), there are masterpieces by Peter Paul Rubens (including "Self-Portrait", "The Head of Medusa"), Albrecht Dürer ("Maximilian I"), Rembrandt ("Self-Portrait"), Van Dyck, Holbein the Younger and Lukas Cranach. A respectable number of masterpieces by Italian, Spanish and French painters, including Titian, Velázquez and **Raphael** (his "Madonna Outdoors" is shown at left) are also represented.

In addition to the artistic handicrafts collection mentioned above, the Museum of Fine Arts also houses an Egyptian collection, a collection of antiques, the "Ambras Portrait Collection" and a coin collection.

One should plan to spend a few days visiting the **Hofburg**, the former Imperial Palace and seat of the Austrian emperors. The complex of buildings found on the enormous tract of land between the Herrengasse, the Augustinergasse and the Ring, represents the architecture of various epochs and contains magnificent rooms and valuable art collections which will fascinate any visitor. Finally completed in 1913, the **New Palace** ("Neue Burg" — shown above) is the most recently built section of the complex. Originally, its architects, Gottfried Semper and Carl Hasenauer, planned that the New Palace comprise one section of an imperial forum, which would be made up of two semi-circular wings stretching toward the Ringstrasse, creating an architectural bond to the Museums of Fine Art and Natural Histroy. (Only the New Palace was ever completed). Today, a large section of the Austrian National Library, diverse collections from the Museum of Fine Arts (weapons, antique musical instruments and the Ephesos Museum), as well as the Ethnological Museum, are found here in this pseudo-Renaissance edifice.

In 1809, the tract in front of the New Palace was deemed a park after the retreating French army had demolished the palace bastion which had occupied that area until then. The Palace Gardens, the new Outer Gate and the Heroes' Square ("Heldenplatz") were also established at that time. Two military equestrian statues, one of Prince Eugene of Savoy (shown on the next page), who defeated the Turks in 1683, the other of Archduke Charles, who was victorious against Napoleon at the Battle of Aspern in 1809 (photo at top of page after next), can also be found on this square.

Construction of the oldest section of the palace complex began in the 13th century during the reign of King Ottocar. The Swiss Courtyard ("Schweizerhof"), at the heart of the complex, was built at that time. Today, the only remnant of the original Gothic structures is provided by the Palace Chapel ("Burgkapelle").

Johann Georg von Hamilton (1672-1737). Neput, a dapplegray, at the gallop, around 1720. Press photographs from the Lipizano Museum.

Anonymous painter. Lipizza Imperial Stables. Early 18th century. Vienna Museum of Fine Art. Press photographs from the Lipizano Museum.

Spanish Riding School. Uniform, two-cornered hat, riding saddle, whip. © Photograph: Henric F. Brabec D'Ipra. Press photographs from the Lipizano Museum.

Johann Georg von Hamilton (1672-1737). White horse from Karst, around 1720. Vienna Museum of Fine Art. Press photographs from the Lipizano Museum.

THE LIPIZANO MUSEUM

The museum is housed on three floors of the former court pharmacy at the Imperial Palace Stables (1st district, Reitschulgasse 2). It looks back at the history of the Lipizzan stallions, and features graceful portraits, riders' uniforms dating from the Hapsburg monarchy, and fascinating facts from the world of haute école. The highlight of the museum is a glimpse at the horses' stables through a soundproof observation window. The shop sells not only equine souvenirs, but also tickets for morning training sessions at the Riding School. Open 9 a.m. to 6 p.m. daily.

Bridle from the gala harness for a team of eight horses from the royal stables, used traditionally by Emperor Francis Joseph at Corpus Christi. Made from gilt brass. Vienna Museum of Fine Art. Press photographs from the Lipizano Museum.

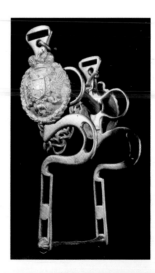

Above: Equestrian statue of Archduke Charles. The "Volksgarten" and the City hall ("Rathaus") can be seen in the background.
Lower left: The official residence of the Austrian president in the Leopold Tract.
Lower right: Parts of the New Palace and the new Outer Palace Gate. In the background, the Museum of Natural History.

The **Swiss Gate** ("Schweizertor" — shown at upper right), with its striking colouration, and the Palace Stables ("Stallburg") both originated during the Renaissance; the Amalia Palace ("Amalienburg") was built somewhat later. These buildings were connected by the early baroque **Leopold Tract** ("Leopoldinischer Trakt"), which serves as the official residence of the Austrian president today (shown on previous page, lower left).

During the extensive baroque remodeling activities which occurred throughout the 18th century, the Imperial Library, the Spanish Riding School and the Imperial Chancellery Tract ("Reichskanzleitrakt") were added to the Imperial Palace. The ceremonial hall, which was built during the early 19th century, served as an international congress centre until a few years ago.

The final addition to the vast imperial complex was the **St. Michael's Tract** ("Michaelertrakt" — pictured above left), which was built according to considerably modified designs by Joseph Emanuel Fischer von Erlach. At the St. Michael's Gate ("Michaelertor"), two monumental wall fountains, the left depicting naval power, the **"Macht zur See"** (lower left), the right showing military strength on land, the "Macht zu Lande", were added.

A memorial to the great composer, Wolfgang Amadeus Mozart, can be found in the Palace Gardens.

The entrance to the **Treasure Chambers** ("Schatzkammer"), which the Hapsburgs filled with invaluable religious and secular objects covering more than a millenium, is located on the Josefsplatz. Among the most impressive objects contained within its walls are the symbols of the Empire, such as the Imperial Crown of Austria (pictured above), which was originally the personal crown of Rudolf II (1552—1612). Austria's first emperor, Francis I, declared it a symbol of state in 1804. Until that time, the Austrian sovereigns were only archdukes of their own territory, while ruling the Holy Roman Empire of German nations. These rulers wore the Imperial Crown (shown at right) which originated in the 10th century.

In the Palace Dining Room, the banquet table is set in the "Supreme Fashion"; as shown, it was only meant for the Emperor Francis Joseph I, closest family members and highest officials. Though no amount of money or effort was spared for representation purposes and outward appearances, the Emperor led a rather ascetic life for a sovereign. Like most of the other rooms in the Palace which are open to the public, his bedroom has been maintained in its original state; it is and was furnished, for instance, with only a simple iron cot (shown at left).

Emperor Francis Joseph I (shown above left) acquired the thrown at the age of eighteen following the Revolution of 1848 and ruled Austria until his death in 1916. His legendary quote: "I am not spared a thing!" was well-founded, both politically and on a private basis. He reigned over an almost unrulable territory comprised of a diversity of peoples and full of explosive elements; though he did not live to see the territory's disintegration, he had envisioned its occurrence. His private life as well was wrought with turns of fate: his beloved wife, the Empress Elisabeth (nicknamed "Sissy"; pictured above) was assassinated in 1898, while their son, Crown Prince Rudolf, committed suicide together with his lover in 1889.

Attending a performance of the Vienna Boys' Choir in the Palace Chapel is an unforgettable experience. This famous choir performs interpretations of masses from Haydn, Mozart, Bruckner and other composers every Sunday and on religious holidays.

The magnificent hall of the **Austrian National Library** is considered the most beautiful library room in the world. In addition to publications, the former Palace Library houses a collection of noteworthy signatures, a map collection and a collection of globes.

The **Spanish Riding School** ("Spanische Hofreitschule") is the only riding school in the world in which the classical form of riding is still practiced. The construction of the building was begun in 1728 according to plans drawn by Fischer von Erlach and completed by his son in 1735. The famous white Lipizzan stallions have been bred in Hapsburg stables since 1580. This Spanish-Arabian breed received its name from the village of Lipizza, in present-day Yugoslavia, the port to which the first horses were brought into southern Europe from Spain. Without witnessing a performance oneself, it is hard to believe that horses, these "Great White Stallions of the Emperor" are indeed capable of performing such elegant movements to the music of minuettes, polkas and slow waltzes.

On December 4, 1883, Austria's Chamber of Deputies and Upper Chamber moved to the new **Parliament** which had been designed by Theophil Hansen and took ten years to complete. The Upper House ("Bundesrat") and Lower House ("Nationalrat") have convened there for more than seventy years. Since 1902, the monumental fountain designed by C. Kundman, with its 13-foot-tall (4 m) statue of *Pallas Athene*, has stood in front of the Parliament building, which covers a roofed area of over 140,000 ft² (13,100 m²).

With this building, architect Theophil Hansen's life-long dream of creating a monumental building in classisistic style became a reality; the Parliament also provides symbolic reference to the "classical" style of democratic government that originated in Greece. In this edifice, the thought that a synthesis of the Greek "polis", a democratic political system, and a constitutional monarchy, would be a possibility, can also be recognized, though at the time of its construction, common voting rights did not yet exist in Austria. The general format of the building, particularly the concept of joining the two Houses of Parliament with a large temple-like atrium, was indeed novel, since such a concept was unknown in antiquity.

Tours of the Parliament building are given regularly except when the Government is in session. (When the Houses convene, flags are flown on the poles at the front of the building).

In 1870, after long negotiations with the Emperor and military forces, Mayor Cajetan Felder was granted the area along the Ring that was used for military drills and parades for the construction of a new **City Hall** ("Rathaus"). Initially, the members of the City Council were not enthusiastic about the idea, but the old City Hall, located on the Wipplingerstrasse, had long since become too small. In 1885, the City Council was finally able to move into the newly built Neo-Gothic City Hall, which had been designed by Friedrich von Schmidt. In addition to the four, over 200-foot-high (61 m), flanking towers, the City Hall possesses a 325-foot (98 m) central tower which is crowned by the almost 10-foot-tall (3 m) copper "Man of the City Hall".

The **Palace Theatre** (or "Burgtheater"), which replaced the National Theatre on the Michaelerplatz after 1888, soon became the most important theatrical stage in German-speaking countries. While the exterior of the theatre, designed by Gottfried Semper and Carl Hasenauer, is Italian High Renaissance, the interior seems almost baroque, particularly the splendid staircase and the ceiling frescoes by Gustav and Ernst Klimt.

As a gesture of gratitude that he survived an assassination attempt, Emperor Francis Joseph I had the **Votive Church** ("Votivkirche") built in 1853. After its consecration on the occasion of the royal pair's silver wedding anniversary (1879), the city of Vienna could claim one of the most outstanding examples of historistic architecture as its own. The church's architect, Heinrich Ferstel, who won the a prize for architecture at the age of 26, imitated the French Gothic cathedral style. The church impresses its viewers with its rich adornment of numerous figurines and the subdued lighting inside that filters through the more than 70 stained glass windows.

The **University of Vienna** was also built according to Ferstel's plans between 1873 and 1883. Its Italian Renaissance style makes the University typical of the monumental buildings on the Ring. Established by Rudolf IV, the Founder, in 1365, it is the oldest university within the German-speaking territories of today. Directly opposite the University is a memorial to a former mayor, Johann Andreas von Liebenberg, who died in 1683 at the head of the students battling against the Turks.

Because Vienna covers a once terraced countryside, small differences in elevation must often be overcome while strolling through its streets. In the suburbs, particularly the Sixth and Ninth Districts, this disadvantage was transformed into a positive feature by constructing numerous, exceptionally attractive pedestrian stairways. One of these, the **"Strudelhof" Steps** (shown at left), gained renown outside the borders of Austria with the novel of the same name written by the Austrian author, Heimito von Doderer.

The Viennese **Museum of Modern Art** ("Museum Moderner Kunst") is actually located in two places. The "Museum of the 20th Century" is used for large, alternating exhibits and the Liechtenstein Palace (pictured below) provides exhibition rooms for permanent collections and smaller alternating exhibits. Among the works in the Palace are pieces by Klimt, Schiele, Picasso, Nolde, Bacon and Beuys.

The Viennese **Stock Exchange** ("Börse"), built between 1874 and 1877 according to plans drawn by Theophil Hansen, suffered heavy damage during World War II. After its reconstruction was finally completed in 1950, the Stock Exchange was destroyed by fire a few years later. During the second period of reconstruction, it was decided that only an inner courtyard should be built instead of rebuilding the original magnificent Exchange Hall with its beautiful coffered ceiling. Following a sort of fairytale trance, the late 1980s saw the revitalization of the Stock Exchange.

The **Rossau Barracks** ("Rossauer Kaserne") also known as the Rudolf Barracks, were constructed in the Windsor style of architecture. Colonel Karl Pihal and Major Karl Markl designed these defensive barracks as a type of arsenal. When the Military moved into the barracks in 1869, they encountered an unpleasant surprise — in planning this edifice, the designers had forgotten the toilets!

First reference to the **"Maria am Gestade"** Church (shown at upper left) was made in 1158. The church's original Romanesque form was destroyed in 1262, the building receiving its present Gothic appearance during in the 14th and 15th centuries.

Built in the first half of the 15th century, the **Citizens' Arsenal** ("Bürgerliches Zeughaus" — shown at upper right), contains the citizens' weapons. Today the building serves a more peaceful purpose, housing the main headquarters of the Vienna Fire Brigade. Originally Gothic in style, the **Church on the Court** ("Kirche am Hof" — shown at lower left), was rebuilt in the baroque style during the 17th century after being destroyed by fire. Henry II resided on this court from 1155 on and it was here that Emperor Francis II announced his renunciation of the German throne in 1806. In October, 1848, the Minister of Defense, Latour, was lynched on a lamppost here by a mob of angry citizens.

Café Central can be counted as one of the most famous coffee houses of the city from which that institution has spread to all corners of the world. The first establishment of this type was the "Zur blauen Flasche", which was opened by Georg Franz Kulczycki (Kolschitzky) on February 27, 1684; he got the idea from the Turks who had beseiged the city the year before.

The Viennese coffee house gradually developed into a popular gathering place for writers, journalists, intellectuals and artists. In the years prior to World War II, Café Central was the favorite haunt of such prominent Viennese authors as Arthur Schnitzler, Karl Kraus, Egon Friedell, and Peter Altenberg, to only mention a few.

The **Danube Canal** has existed as a regulated arm of the Danube River since 1598. It has a length of around 10.6 miles (17 kilometres) and divides the First District from the Second. A particularly pleasant pastime, day or night, is a cruise of the Danube Canal, starting from either of its banks, and enjoying the city from the deck or restaurant of one of the many excursion boats.

The **Wedding Fountain** ("Vermählungsbrunnen" — shown on the right), is found on the Hohe Markt, Vienna's oldest square and the focal point of city life during the Middle Ages. The palace of the Roman defense commander was also located here; Marcus Aurelius resided in its rooms for many years, passing away in that building in 180 AD. Later, the City Court (the "Schranne"), the "Narrenkotter", (cages in which troublemakers, ruffians, drunkards, "shameless whores", magicians and fortune-tellers were subjected to public ridicule) and the pillary (1710—1848), were all located at this site. Emperor Leopold I made an oath to have a fountain dedicated to St. Joseph built, should his eldest son, Joseph I, be successful in capturing the fortress of Laudon and return home safely. The first version of the fountain, designed by Johann Bernhard Fischer von Erlach and constructed of wood, did not survive long. Emperor Charles VI had the original fountain removed in 1725 and a new one built of marble and iron according to designs drawn by Joseph Emanuel Fischer von Erlach; the bronze temple honouring St. Mary's wedding is supported by four Corinthian columns.

The Anker Clock (shown below) "hangs" suspended between the **Anker House** (at Hoher Markt No. 11) and the building at Hoher Markt No. 10, and was constructed according to designs created by the painter, Franz von Matsch. Every day at noon, spectators can watch as its figurines parade across the face of the clock.

St. Ruprecht's Church ("Ruprechtskirche") is Vienna's oldest religious structure. According to oral tradition, it was built in the middle of the 8th century at the site where two Christian apostles, Cunald and Gisalrich, had established a subterranean house of worship. It is more likely that the church was actually built in the 11th century; the first documented mention of this edifice was made in 1161. Its present appearance was given to this church during the 12th and 13th centuries, where it stood on a rise, free to all sides, in the oldest section of the city.

A member of the aristocracy, Georg von Auersperg, financed the renovation of the church in 1436/37. In fact, "this pitiful little church played no other role in the history of the city than repeatedly undergoing restoration work" (Groner). Emperor Ferdinand I turned the St. Ruprecht's Church over to the Franciscan Brotherhood in 1533, though they only took care of it for a period of twelve years. Over the last four centuries, the church has been renovated, restored and remodeled at least a dozen times. In 1708, an altar piece created by the famous baroque painter, Johann Michael Rottmayr, was donated to the church. During its 1837 restoration, some Gothic features were added. In addition to an organ loft with figured tracery parapets from the year 1439 and a Gothic holy-water font (from around 1500), the stained glass windows created by G. S. Mohn (1824) and H. Tahedl (1933—34) are also worthy of attention.

According to legend, Augustine, the popular folksinger, often frequented the **"Griechenbeisl"**, where he supposedly also composed and presented the beloved song, "O, du lieber Augustin, alles ist hin!" to an audience for the first time. In those days, the establishment was known as the "Reichenbergbeisl" and was the favourite haunt of the Reichenberg cloth merchants. The main medieval structure, built on a narrow, deep plot of land, is Gothic and originated in the 15th century. The late-Gothic bay and the facade were transformed and rebuilt in baroque style in 1709 and 1784 respectively. This restaurant has been known as the "Griechenbeisl" since the 18th century and could welcome such prominent guests as Wagner, Strauss, Brahms, Grillparzer, Nestroy and Lueger on a regular basis.

But the "Griechenbeisl" is by no means the only establishment of its kind in this section of town. In recent years, the area between this building and the St. Ruprecht's Church has become known as the "Bermuda Triangle", since evening visitors, once there, have been known to disappear for a longer time than intended in one or more of the many bars, jazz clubs, cafés and discotheques the district offers.

Next to the "Griechenbeisl", one can find the Greek Non-Uniate Church. The Byzantine-style basilica is built of red and yellow bricks and is known locally as the "Golden House", since all ornaments (of fired clay) are gold-plated.

The **Giant Ferris Wheel** ("Riesenrad"), is Vienna's second most famous landmark next to St. Stephen's Cathedral. During the slow, relaxing ride, one can enjoy a tremendous view of the city below from this unusual attraction which was built in 1896/97 in the Prater Park. The structure suffered severe fire damage during World War II and all carriages were destroyed.

The Prater is considered one of the largest recreational areas of the city. In addition to the "Wurstelprater", the amusement park, spacious grassy areas invite one to spend one's leisure time there. Earlier, only the aristocracy had access to the Prater. In 1592, Rudolf II transferred the authority to determine who had the right to enter the Prater to the Imperial Woodsman, Hans Bengel, who utilized such unsophisticated and rude manners in fulfilling this duty that the name "Bengel" is still used today as an insult in Austria.

Emperor Joseph II opened the Prater to the public in 1765. One of the most enjoyable ways of viewing this large park is by taking a ride on the **Lilliput Steamtrain,** which travels along 2.5 miles (4 kilometres) of narrow-gauge track past the park's major attractions.

The **"Wurstelprater"**, or amusement park, can fulfill any child's wildest desire — dungeons and ghost train rides, carousels, auto-dromes, elevated sightseeing rides, shooting galleries, crazy houses, giant ship swings, and much more. What better excuse than taking care of the kids could a parent have for a few care-free hours of enjoyment. And for those who are un-able to persuade their youngsters that it's time to go, the "Watschenmann", a life-size punching dummy, can be used for a few coins to get rid of their excess energy.

A new era in communal living — particularly with regard to the exteriors of conventional social housing units — was introduced by the so-called **"Hundertwasser House"**, located on the Löwengasse in the Third District. The plans for the building were created by Friedensreich Hundertwasser, who has been considered one of Austria's leading artists for some time. His apartment house, which reminds one of his colourful, typically spiral-dominated paintings, was established to meet the need for humane and comfortable living accommodations in an urban environment.

Such an impression is certainly created when one looks at the originality of the house's exterior; the building's interior has remained rather traditional. The house is difficult to categorize according to architectural style, though it tends to remind one of the works carried out by the Spanish *art nouveau* architect, Gaudi. One also senses the fact that Vienna was the "breeding ground" of the baroque, and the frivolity of that era seems to have influenced Hundertwasser as well. The building is characterized by the avoidance of straight lines and large cubes to a great extent, by the bright colours of the interwoven constructional elements and by furnishing the horizontal surfaces with bushes, trees and other plants.

After renters moved into the house in 1986, this building became a primary tourist attraction within an extremely short time. As a result, the quality of living declined tremendously, since the streets in the vicinity are usually blocked by buses and empty parking spaces are a scarcity in this area. Noise and smog pollution is a high price for the residents of the Hundertwasser House to pay for the originality of their domicile. Hope remains that the urban waste incineration plant, which is being designed by Hundertwasser at the moment, will draw at least some of the attention away from their house.

Millions of television screens in almost every Western nation show the same picture on the first day of the New Year, when the Vienna Philharmonic Orchestra presents its legendary New Year's Day concert from the Grand Hall of the **Viennese Music Society House** ("Musikvereinsgebäude"). The great number of viewers could compete easily with that for Grand Prix auto races. The Music Society serves as the heart of Viennese concert life throughout the year as well. The Grand Hall can seat an audience of 2000 and its acoustics have given it the reputation of being the best concert hall in the world.

The original "Viennese Society of Music Friends" was founded in 1812; they assigned Theophil Hansen the planning of "their" building in the 1860s. The first concert in the classically furnished Renaissance-style concert house was held on January 6, 1870. Of interest and importance for the music world are the Society's extensive archives, where as yet unpublished works of famous musicians can still be found.

Located between the Inner City and the Vienna River, the City Park ("Stadtpark") stretches along the one-time water glacis. With landscaping similar to an English estate, this park was opened to the public in 1862. The "Kursalon" (shown above) was built in Italian Renaissance style according to plans drawn by the architect, Johann Garben, between 1865 and 1867 and is used for cultural purposes, primarily concerts.

Only a few steps away, one can find a memorial to a composer whose melodies are beloved the world over. The bronze statue of Johann Strauss (son), the "Waltz King", stands in front of a graceful carved marble arch. Strauss' "Blue Danube Waltz" (which proved a flop at its premiere in 1867), has become Vienna's theme song, and many of his operettas, particularly "The Fledermaus" and "The Zigeunerbaron", have become world-famous.

The **Belvedere Palace** was built by Prince Eugene of Savoy at the beginning of the 18th century and is situated on a rise south of the central city. The opulent, elaborate structures and grounds and the elevated site (literally reigning above the Hofburg), not only reflect his tremendous financial strength but also the social status this prince enjoyed. After Vienna's liberation from the Turks, in which Prince Eugene played a considerable role, he became especially beloved by the people of the city. In fact, he was so popular that the decision made in 1697 to take the command of the Imperial Army from him had to be reversed due to the pressure placed on the decision-makers by the Viennese. His palace represents a masterpiece of sophisticated baroque architecture; Johann Lukas von Hildebrandt was responsible for its planning and design. The artistic gardens and park were created by the Bavarian landscape architect, Dominique Girard. The State Treaty, which released Austria from its 10-year-long occupation, was signed in the Belvedere Palace on May 15, 1955.

Prince Eugene resided primarily in the Lower Belvedere, since that section was closer to the city and was somewhat smaller than the Upper Palace. In the latter, elaborate festivities were celebrated — not only during the Prince's lifetime, but long thereafter, for instance, during the Congress of Vienna (1814/15). Later, Anton Bruckner also lived in the servants' tract until his death, and Chancellor Schuschnigg moved his official residence there in 1934.

Today, the **Gallery of the 19th and 20th Centuries** is housed in the Upper Belvedere. In addition to a large collection of Biedermeier and Romance-period art, the most well-known paintings of Austrian turn-of-the-century artists are on exhibit. Two artists of that era became world-famous: Gustav Klimt — his paintings, "The Kiss" (shown above) and "Judith", as well as many of his other renowned works, are exhibited in the Belvedere — and Egon Schiele, the "enfant terrible" of the Viennese art scene.

The **St. Charles Church** ("Karlskirche") is the most important religious baroque structure in Vienna, and represents Johann Bernhard Fischer von Erlach's architecturally creative heyday. During the Plague years, Emperor Charles VI made an oath to the patron saint of pestilence, St. Charles Borromeo, to build a splendid church; he fulfilled his promise generously after the end of the Plague. The Crown Territories were also asked to contribute to the financing of the construction work, which cost around 304,000 guldens; the "House of God" was consecrated in 1738. The edifice architecturally combines the elements of classical architecture (Greek, Roman and Byzantine components are evident) in a genial manner. The reliefs on the almost 160-ft-high (47 m) columns show scenes taken from the life of St. Charles. Before other structures were built on the grounds in front of the church, optical effects from a distance made it appear even larger from the front.

The creative decorations and artwork in the interior of the church were carried out by Joseph Emanuel, the son of J. B. Fischer von Erlach, who passed away in 1723. The frescoes in the cupola, painted by Johann Michael Rottmayr, seem to dominate the interior, and the cupola's oval shape makes it appear even higher than it is in actuality by means of optical illusion. There are also numerous baroque masterpieces, for instance by Daniel Gran and Martin Altmonte. Despite these touches of colour, the St. Charles Church maintains a cool atmosphere within, particularly in comparison to its exterior.

The **"Liberation Monument"** ("Befreiungsdenkmal") was a gift of the Soviet Union to the City of Vienna, which, during the Russian Occupation following the Second World War, assumed responsibility for the monument's maintenance. The monument, called simply the "Russian Monument" by the local residents, was intended as a memorial to the soldiers of the Red Army who were killed during the battle to free Vienna in 1945.

Another type of monument is presented by the **Urban Train stations** ("Stadtbahnstationen") designed by Otto Wagner (1841–1918), one of Vienna's most renowned architects. They are considered some of the most beautiful examples of *art nouveau* ("Jugendstil") architecture, built during an era which influenced the appearance of this city quite significantly.

The centre of artists of the *art nouveau* period was the **Secession** (upper photo), which was built by Joseph Maria Olbrich (1897/98) in a style which was revolutionary for that time. This building paved the way for a new style of architecture, which oriented itself around clear cubic forms and incorporated ornamentation deliberately to emphasize architectural thoughts. Features of the Secession which deserve special mention are the heavy metal doors (designed by Gustav Klimt) and the cupola of gold-plated laurel branches, which is known as the "Krauthappl" (transl.: head of cabbage) by the local residents.

Otto Wagner was **the** *art nouveau* architect. Two of his houses, located on the Wienzeile, which display particularly elaborate *art nouveau* ornamentation, are the **Majolikahaus** (opposite page, lower left) with its original facade, and its neighbor (opposite page, lower right), decorated with gold-plated medallions designed by the *art nouveau* artist, Kolo Moser. Despite the progressive nature of the latter buildings, these buildings remind one of he spirit of the baroque era, which shared the dainty ornateness and excessive ornamentation of the *art nouveau* period. Built between 1904 and 1907, the **church** that Wagner created for the psychiatric asylum **"Am Steinhof"** (upper left) became the major ecclesiastical structure of the Viennese *art nouveau* era. Ernst Fuchs, one of Austria's well-known modern artists, resides in one of Wagner's villas (upper right) today.

Art nouveau ornamentation in the Inner City

Art nouveau house on the Wienzeile

One of the most famous of Vienna's attractions is **Schönbrunn Palace** ("Schloss Schönbrunn") on the west side of the city. The beautifully laid out palace grounds, now a park, cover more than four times the area of Vatican City. Originally, the "Katter Mill" occupied this site from the 14th century on; the "Katter Castle" adjacent to the mill was acquired by Emperor Maximilian II in 1569, who remodeled it into a hunting lodge. This lodge was then burnt down by the Hungarians in 1605. Emperor Matthias, who also discovered the beautiful springs, where later the lovely fountains or "schönen Brunnen" for which the palace was named were found, had the lodge rebuilt.

After the Turks burnt the lodge down again in 1683, Emperor Leopold I decided to build a new summer residence for himself and his son, Joseph I. The initial design by Johann Bernhard Fischer von Erlach planned that the palace be built on the rise on which the Gloriette was finally constructed (shown in background in upper photo on opposite page, and below). Instead of carrying out these plans, which would have resulted in a royal residence far surpassing Versailles in grandeur and furnishings, new designs were made and construction of the palace began on its present site; the basic structure was completed in 1700.

Emperor Charles VI preferred the Favorita, the Hapsburg's old summer residence, to Schönbrunn Palace. The former was, however, avoided by Empress Maria Theresia after her father's death, and considerable additions were made to Schönbrunn Palace between 1744 and 1749, whereby the original rococo style was maintained throughout the interior. As of 1765, Joseph II hosted splendid festivities in the palace. The impressive **Gloriette** was completed in 1775; in those early days, it possessed gigantic windows and served as the site for innumerable social events. One has a tremedous view of the city from the Gloriette.

Both in 1805 and in 1809, Napoleon Bonaparte resided in these beautifully furnished rooms. Emperor Francis I had the facades altered between 1816 and 1819. After that, Schönbrunn Palace served as the permanent summer residence of the Austrian Imperial Family. Emperor Francis Joseph I, who was born in the palace in 1830 and died there in 1916, replaced all empire-style furnishings with those of rococo. Emperor Charles I laid down the Imperial Crown at Schönbrunn in 1918.

The 42 rooms of the palace which are open to the public are well worth seeing. The **Grand Ballroom** (opposite, upper left) provided an elegant setting for festive dinners and balls which took place during the Monarchy. The walls of the **Gobelin Room** (opposite, lower left) are hung with three 18th-century tapestries from Brussels. Scenes depicting the twelve months of the year are woven into the backs and seats of the six armchairs found there. **Emperor Francis Joseph I's bedroom** was intentionally kept simple and plain (upper photo); only the two paintings by Franz von Matsch ("Pledge of Allegiance from the German Princes" and "Emperor Francis Joseph's Deathbed") serve as decoration. The **Palace Theatre** (lower photo) is Vienna's only remaining baroque theatre.

Above: The Imperial Carriage, one of the 130 vehicles which comprise the largest carriage collection of the world.
Left: The "schöne Brunnen" (transl.: beautiful fountain) from which the Palace received its name.
Below: The Palm House

In 1752, Empress Maria Theresia made the decision to establish a **zoological garden** on the Schönbrunn Palace grounds. Not only its unusual circular shape but the multitude of animal species which can be found there make this zoo a truly remarkable facility. At the moment, the enclosures are undergoing long overdue remodeling to meet modern animal-keeping requirements; nevertheless, visitors may stroll freely through the zoo.

When one sees a cluster of fir twigs hanging above the door of one of the inns in the Viennese suburbs of Grinzing, Sievering, Heiligenstadt or Nussdorf, one knows that that year's wine is ready to be enjoyed. The unique atmosphere to be found in the "Heurigen" localities is world-famous, though one must look around a bit to find it in a relatively unadulterated form.

The Viennese themselves are avid visitors of these traditional institutions. The new "Heurigen" wine, which can only originate in the innkeeper's own vineyards, "enjoys such popularity, that the Viennese stroll out to Grinzing in herds to consume that wine in the many "Heurigen" localities, and which is known to produce local minstrels as well." (Groner: *Vienna, as it was; 1934*). "Heurigen" music is almost as well-known as the associated "grape juice". In most wine-restaurants, the traditional quartette of two violins, accordion and guitar reproduce the melodies of the Schrammel brothers, who gave their name to the type of music found here.

The house in which Beethoven died.

From the **Kahlenberg**, Vienna's highest point, one has a outstanding view over the city. The photo above shows the island ("Donauinsel") separating the Danube River from the relief channel; the island is a popular site for sun bathers, strollers and windsurfers throughout the summer months.

King John III **Sobieski** of Poland and his army departed from the Kahlenberg in 1683 to fight against the Turks which held the city, together with Austrian, Bavarian and Saxon troops (lower left). Legend has it that Sobieski prayed for God's support in the **Church on the Kahlenberg** (lower right) before that battle.

The **Danube Tower** ("Donauturm"), with a height of almost 832 feet (252 metres) is Austria's highest structure. On clear days, one can see the Hungarian border from the restaurant which slowly rotates at an elevation of 561 feet (170 metres).

One of the most modern bridges of Vienna spans the Danube River at the site where the ancient **Reich's Bridge** ("Reichsbrücke"), which collapsed in 1976, once stood.

In the years following the Second World War, Vienna became one of the most important meeting places between East and West, partially due to its advantageous geographical location and partially because of Austria's politically neutral status. In addition to being the site of summit meetings between the Superpowers, Vienna is also the site chosen for the continuing Strategic Arms Limitations Talks. Despite its being the subject of vehement domestic political discussions, a separate convention centre, the "Austria Center Vienna", shown in the foreground above, was built directly adjacent to the Vienna International Centre ("UNO City") to house that and other conferences. A bit of additional information — In 1987, the SALT II participants had to be persuaded by the Austrian Chancellor himself to vacate the prestigious rooms which they had occupied in the Hofburg Palace up to that point and to move to the new Austria Center. He was only successful because the congress centre is directly accessible by subway and lies within a large park area near the Danube Island recreational district.

Since 1979, Vienna has served as the third seat of the United Nations, in addition to New York and Geneva, though several special organizations such as the International Atomic Energy Organization (IEAO), the United Nations Industrial Development Organization (UNIDO), as well as the U. N. Relief and Works Agency for Palastinian Refugees in the Near East (UNRWA) and the Centre for Social Development and Human Affairs (CSDHA), established their headquarters in Vienna previously. The Republic of Austria and the City of Vienna established the Austrian International Centre on extraterritorial ground; the buildings, which are visible for a great distance, are rented to the United Nations Organization for the symbolic amount of 1 Austrian Schilling per year.

Not far distant from the International Centre, eight Islamic nations established Vienna's first **Islamic Centre** (lower photo) with funds provided by the King of Saudi Arabia reigning at that same time.

Near **Hinterbrühl,** close to Mödling at the southern city limits of Vienna, one can find Europe's largest subterranean lake, which has a surface area of around 67,800 ft² (6300 m²). In earlier times, a gypsum mine had been worked at Hinterbrühl, but in 1912, a spring was exposed during dynamiting work and water gradually filled the cavern with around 71 million cubic feet (20 million hectolitres) of water. From 1932 on, guided boat tours have attracted innumerable visitors. During the Second World War, the Heinkel Company established an underground aeroplane factory in the grotto.

SISI
Empress of Austria
Queen of Hungary
1837–1898

Elisabeth Amalie Eugenie von Wittelsbach (Sisi) was born in Munich on December 24, 1837. She was the fourth child of Duke Maximilian and his wife Maria Ludovica (née Princess of Bavaria and sister of Archduchess Sophie). She spent her youth at Possenhofen Castle in Bavaria and was an unconventional, freedom-loving, truth-loving and sensitive girl.

Originally, Francis Joseph was supposed to marry her elder sister, Helene. Such, at least, was the plan of the two sisters, Archduchess Sophie and Ludovica. However, Francis Joseph fell in love with Elisabeth, nicknamed Sisi. Their betrothal was made public in Bad Ischl on August 19, 1853. The wedding was set for April 9, 1854.

Sisi become enmeshed in the intrigues of her mother-in-law and the court nobility of Vienna. She gave birth to 4 children: Sophie (1855–1857), Gisela (1856–1892), Crown Prince Rudolph (1858–1889) and Marie Valerie (1868–1924). After Archduchess Sophie took Sisi's children away from her, bitter struggles ensued.

Sisi left Vienna in the summer of 1860 and engaged in travels during the following two years. In 1862, she returned to the capital city.

On June 8, 1867, Emperor Francis Joseph was crowned Apostolic King of Hungary and Elisabeth, Queen of Hungary. The coronation ceremonies took place in the Matthiaskirche zu Ofen in Budapest.

Elisabeth displayed little interest in politics. Nonetheless, she achieved the reconciliation with Hungary in 1866/67. Francis Joseph built the Hermes Villa in Vienna for her.

The suicide of Rudolph (1889) in Mayerling, her youthful infatuation with Ludwig II. of Bavaria, her unhappy marriage, her life of travels and her murder all made her a popular figure of novels and films (3 Sisi movies). The musical "Elisabeth", which premiered at the Theater an der Wien on September 3, 1992, was also extremely successful.

Ceremonial reception of Her Royal Highness at the Elisabeth Bridge on April 3, 1854. Joseph Haydn composed the folk hymn (Kaiserhymne). The text was composed by Johann Gabriel Seidl.

Austria's most wondrous day. The Cardinal presents the rings to the bridal couple. Wedding on April 24, 1854 in the Augustiner Hofkirche.

Francis Joseph shows Sisi the city of Vienna.

Emperor's villa in Bad Ischl

Hermes Villa – a gift from Emperor Francis Joseph to Empress Elisabeth (1882–1886)

Elisabeth at the beginning of her 3rd decade of life
Lithograph by Adolf Doulhage

COAT-OF-ARMS OF HIS MAJESTY THE EMPEROR

COAT-OF-ARMS OF HER MAJESTY THE EMPRESS